Dragonfly Tea

Dog-eared

D.L. Lang

Dragonfly Tomorrows & Dog-eared Yesterdays

D.L. Lang

Copyright © 2017 Diana L. Lang

All rights reserved. No part of this publication may be reproduced, distributed, or transmitted in any form or by any means, including photocopying, recording, or other electronic or mechanical methods, without the prior written permission of the publisher, except in the case of brief quotations embodied in critical reviews and certain other noncommercial uses permitted by copyright law. For permission requests, write to the author at the email address below:
poetryebook@gmail.com
poetryebook.com

ISBN-13:978-1548437725
ISBN-10: 1548437727

About the Poet

In addition to the book you are holding in your hands, Diana L. Lang of Vallejo, CA is the author of *Tea & Sprockets, Abundant Sparks & Personal Archeology, Look Ma! No Hands!, Poet Loiterer, Id Biscuits, Barefoot in the Sanctuary,* and *Armor Against The Dawn.* She also released her debut spoken word album entitled *Happy Accidents.* Her work has also been published in the *Benicia Herald* and the *Jewish Journal of Los Angeles.*

She was recently named Poet Laureate of Vallejo, California for 2017-2019.

Find D.L. Lang online at
Twitter/Instagram: @poetryebook
Facebook: http://www.facebook.com/DinahLLang
http://www.poetryebook.com
poetryebook@gmail.com

Gratitude

This book is dedicated to Tim, *basherti,*
for his love, support, and caring for me.

Thank you to the 2017 Alameda County Fair for awarding
"Expectations of a Future" a Silver Award.

The following poems which appear in this book won awards in
creative writing at the 2017 Marin County Fair:

"The Sixties", First Place in Flashback to the 60's Poetry
"Lift Off!", First Place in Fair Themed Poetry
"Street Mouse", Second Place in Any other Haiku
"Sally", Third Place in My Pet

My deepest gratitude to the judges.

A huge thanks to local photographer, Jessica Brown, who shot the
cover image for this book!

I am truly grateful that you chose to buy this book.
If you enjoyed it, please take the time to review it.

Peace and love to all who read it.

Foreword

Dragonfly Tomorrows & Dog-eared Yesterdays is my 9th poetry collection comprised of poems that were written between December 2016 and June 2017. The title came about as I was stopped at a red light. A local restaurant had a sign on the corner that said, "Catfish Today," so as a way of passing the time I broke down those words and came up with additional phrases that contained a compound word with an animal and a time period.

My aim with this book was to try to largely be uplifting and distracting as an antidote to the often heartbreaking chaos of the world today, so there are intentionally less topical poems than in previous collections. My two personal favorites of this variety are "Where are the Heroes?" and "Affirmations of a Dream" which close out the book. "Cats on Caravan" and "IWWD" refer to my experience of the Women's March and Strike.

As I was preparing my entries for area fairs this year, I wrote "Lift Off!" describing the experience of the fair. "The Sixties" was written to fit the theme of the Marin County Fair that is honoring the 50th anniversary of the Summer of Love. I was not alive in those years, obviously, but tried to write from the perspective of someone who was. It is one period in American history that continues to fascinate me. I'm quite pleased that both were awarded blue ribbons.

I also spent a lot of time reminiscing about my childhood haunt in Enid, Oklahoma, a field down by the railroad tracks that's now called Oakwood Nature Park, so "Blanton-Kiowa Line" captures the history of that area. I named the wrong trail in the original poem. This version fixes that error. I've developed an affinity for train songs, so my husband challenged me to write "Hanukah Train" as we found ourselves listening to old folk songs this past Hanukah.

This volume brings the total of my published poems to 918. While it will be the first book released after being named the 2nd Poet Laureate of Vallejo, California, poems written during that tenure will be released in future books. This milestone provides a natural closing point for this book.

Thanks for reading!

The Front Cover Concept

A penguin superhero in a pose of strength with a sign that says "Save the Humans!"

I have an affinity for penguins, and whenever someone gifts me a penguin toy, my husband and I often joke about how the membership of a fictional group called the Penguin Liberation Front has grown. This fictional group frees penguins from captivity, whether real or artistic representations.

The cape is also a reference to a song that Dan Nichols sang to me in 2015.

The railroad tracks overgrown with wild brush represent both the past, and my affinity for trains which shows up in many poems both in this book and past books.

Jessica Brown brought this vision to life, shooting the cover photo and author photo with me in costume on a very humid August 3rd, 2017 at the Mare Island Nature Preserve in Vallejo. Although as a child I often wandered live railroad tracks in Oklahoma, these tracks were no longer in use, so it was safe to stand upon them.

Table of Poetry

Expectations of a Future 1
Wildflowers 2
Dog-eared Yesterdays 3
Balcony Dreams 4
Celestial Scenes 5
A Pillow for the Heart 6
There are 7
Holy Stumblings 8
Spring in the City 9
Choose to Be 10
Parallels 11
And If They Can, Why Can't We? 12
At the Intersection 13
There's a Peace in Slowness 15
How to Read Poetry 16
The Seeker 17
Happy Place 18
Those of Gentle Hearts 19
Traffic Jammer 20
Birds in Harmony 21
Each One of Us 22
Dreams Demand 23
Go Down Easy 24
Yes 25
A Circle of Dreams 26
The Sixties 27
Lift Off! 29
Dixon May Fair 30
Waterfront Observations 31
Island Poem 32
Generation Transformation 33
All I've Got Left of You 34
Time Overdrawn 35
Bright Light 36
Hanukah Train 37

Blanton-Kiowa Line	38
Enid	40
Sunrise	41
Praying for Rain	42
April Foolery	44
Anytime	45
Hang On to Your Soul	46
Sally	47
The Talebearer	48
Zing	49
A Home	50
One Two	51
Somewhere Beyond	52
Personal Evolution	53
Like Broken Glass	54
Moments	55
Old Songs	56
Sparked by Melody	57
Renewed	58
Awe	59
As the Sun	60
Street Mouse	61
Class Participation	62
Beachside	63
A Napa Moment	64
Mall Walker	65
epic history poem	66
Antisocial Media	71
The Way to Contentment	72
Humanity	73
Brightest	74
Greed's Disconnect	75
Although	77
Ochlocracy	78
Politics	79
This Earth Day	80
Stay Lit	81

On Fear 82
Lines 83
Dear Land of the Free 86
IWWD 87
What if? 88
Radioactive Returns 89
Cats on Caravan 91
New Old America 92
Immigrants' Truth 93
What's It Gonna Take? 94
Not Your Problem? 95
You Cannot See Through Gold 96
Where are the Heroes? 98
Affirmations of a Dream 99

Dragonfly Tomorrows & Dog-eared Yesterdays
D.L. Lang

Expectations of a Future

We are but overgrown children,
souls colliding,
trained in a time that no longer exists
for a world that never will,
stumbling through our days
with outdated road maps,
clinging to memories
of a previous normality,
encountering the fallacies
of an unpredictable future,
learning to bounce.

Wildflowers

Like wildflowers at roadside
you've a passion you cannot hide.

A splash of rainbow in seas of gray
calmly blooming above the fray
no matter what chaos comes your way.

Dog-eared Yesterdays

Beyond the shooting stars,
across roaring rivers,
over the potato slough.

Moonlight halo in the starlight.
The time is now.
It's gonna be all right.

The daydreams
cycle into night dreams.

Kept awake by happy memories,
giggling and giddy
with thoughts of dragonfly tomorrows,
nestled in the boxes of
dog-eared yesterdays,
and nights strung together
by melodies.

Balcony Dreams

Twinkle, twinkle little satellite,
how I wonder where you're at tonight.
Vibrations of the heavens so bright.

A whirligig smiling in the night,
riding a sunflower propeller,
hanging onto a hot air balloon
illuminated by paper lanterns.

Celestial Scenes

We dance upon these fields of green,
twirling beneath celestial scenes,

drinking in skies of brilliant blue,
as birds they soar in every hue,

singing their rhymes up to the moon,
performing love songs for me and you

as sweet and bright as any fruit
picked fresh from orchards newly a bloom.

A Pillow for the Heart

When I think of all the miles
spent walking in the country sides,
I lean my head back and smile,
for joy's impossible to hide.

A solitary momentary memory
cast forth into my vision
coloring everything I see
with attitudes delicious.

I'm looking for a pathway
back to just how I felt before,
but feelings've got a way
of closing down the door.

I cling on to these stories
to lift myself up when it's hard—
a distraction from my worries
like a pillow for the heart.

There are...

There are songs
that only the ocean can sing.
There are poems
that only the flowers can write.

There are paintings
that only the sun can create.
There are plays
that only the animals recite.

There are spaces
that only a mountain can design.
There are sculptures
that only the river can mold.

There are dreams
that only grow upon the trees.

Yet humans see something
that can only be sold.

Holy Stumblings

It is overcast
as I sit upon the balcony,
thinking about the past,
drinking tea,
pondering life's mystery.

Life is a series
of holy stumblings
and divine redirections.

You walk a path
and start tumbling,
uncovering your own heart,
and remembering
what it's always longed for.

You find your purpose,
viewed in reverse,
while stumbling forward
across stepping stones
of gratitude.

Spring in the City

Above the rush
of the highway,
I hear them singing—
nestled in trees,
relaxing.

The birds have returned
from journeys afar,
carrying melodies,
announcing:

"It is spring.
It is spring.

Won't you join in?

Leave your houses
and just sing."

Choose to Be

When's the last time you rose to your feet,
swept up by excitement over someone sweet?

Can you recall the crescendo of the seas
that once brought you right down to your knees?

Do you remember feeling so wonderfully free
upon ascending majestic towering trees?

Have they walled you in with the concrete,
so your life shall remain so orderly and neat?

When last did you wander unfamiliar streets,
truly curious about everyone you'll meet?

Arise! Arise from your well-worn seat,
and follow the drumming of your heartbeat!

There awaits a fabulous world for you to see
with a new evolution of who you shall be,
each and every day, be you one or ninety,
if only, if only, you will choose to be thee!

Parallels

We're all drunk on stories.

A romanticized past
passed down
from legend to novice.

Cosmic conversations
of conscious comrades
creating converts.

Remembering, recreating,
reconstituting the ingredients
of magic histories
of some past beatnik bohemia
that we wish we'd lived.

Blurring these
with memories
of the heights we've reached.

Creating new mythologies
blended with our dreams,
searching for alignment.

We are left awestruck
upon arrival.

And If They Can, Why Can't We?

The sun drips through the greenery
as critters scamper beneath the trees.

The marble sand melts into the sea
as birds soar high—so wild and free.

Vines grow beyond fences easily,
ignoring every boundary.

I drink in this blessed scenery
while pondering my humanity.

Dragonfly Tomorrows & Dog-eared Yesterdays
D.L. Lang

At the Intersection

Rocking out. Rocking there.
Rocking out in my rocking chair.
The chorus in my head's gone on parade.
Songs of youth never show their age.

My head transports to my European youth,
as I stood up there in my hiking shoes,
gazing down at orange topped roofs
nestled in valleys of wild green grasses.

Taking a twisting trail through time,
searching for something genuine,
as the road just winds and winds
on footpaths dotted with flowery patches.

Elevation clears a heavy mind.
It's all right. Just take your time.
There's a whole world for you to find.
Only your heart knows what the right path is.

He hired a transcriptionist
to take down his mind
of all that he may dream
on a night like this.

Bubbles, lava lamps, dust bunnies.
Walking in circles. Trying to get free.
The eyes see what they want to see.
His eyes see words of poetry.

Poetry oft arrives after midnight
after flying high as a kite
from some far off starry light
to shout rhymes with all its might.

Dragonfly Tomorrows & Dog-eared Yesterdays
D.L. Lang

The muse rarely awakens in the day,
preferring not to ever say
what soft dreams it wishes to lay
until the sunset guides the way.

Blowing smoke rings at the sun.
C'mon now. Tell 'em what you've done.
Trying to break free from the feedback loop.
Every tongue's got an opinion on the scoop.

We're moving in the wrong direction.
We'll need to turn right back around.
We're all looking for perfection,
but there is none to be found.

When I knew nothing of this world,
I invented worlds of my own—
elaborate youthful fantasies
to make sense of what's unfurled,

but now as I am growing old,
I admit I know so little still,
for life means so much more
than just a search for gold.

I'll meet you at the intersection
where life's a bit more interesting
just beyond the battles and protesting
where a man can find some freedom.

There's a Peace in Slowness

When last did you sit and stare
at the sparkling evening sky,
gazing up without a care,
content with not knowing why?

When last did your eyes examine
a painting so close that you
could so perfectly imagine
walking within its milieu?

How to Read Poetry

Poetry is meant to be read with the heart,
yet academics wish to pick the verses apart.
You wouldn't unravel your favorite sweater,
so why reduce poems back down to each letter?

Disassembling a recipe to its ingredients
may help you learn about the process,
but that was never how the chef meant
his life's work to be digested.

Poetry is an experience that must be felt.
It's a coping mechanism for what life has dealt.
It's meant to give you brief respite from the pain.
Your heart understands why more so than your brain.

The mind tries to organize and categorize
into useful or useless, truth or lies,
what to forget and what to remember,
reducing the fire back down to its embers.

The heart just takes the whole picture inside,
whispering notions that lie between the lines.
Where the mind sees only languages,
the heart sees the work of paint brushes.

Poetry isn't meant to be taken so literally.
There's rarely any practical applicability.
If you wish to understand poetry,
then you must let go and just let it be.

Only then can you truly see
what exists right here between you and me.

The Seeker

I'm just looking for the answers
in every song that I sing.
I'm just looking for answers
in what the brand new day will bring.

I'm just looking for the answers,
as I stroll upon this street.
I'm just looking for the answers
from every soul that I meet.

I'm just looking for the answers
'bout why this world's so unkind.
All I'm finding is more questions
that leave my head all in a bind.

I'm just looking for the answers
in every book that I may read.
I'm just looking for the answers
no matter where the day may lead.

I'm just looking for the answers,
but I don't know what I'll find.
All I'm finding is more questions
keep on flooding across my mind.

I'm just looking for the answers
while gazing at these starry nights.
I'm just looking for the answers
that'll just make everything all right.

I'm just looking for the answers
to these questions that do cry,
and I'll be looking for the answers
'til the very day that I die.

Happy Place

Your songs shield my soul
from life's storms.

When you play
the joy in your eyes
is its own symphony.

My heart hears
the words in languages
that my tongue cannot translate.

Your voice is my happy place.
Thanks for the trip.

Those of Gentle Hearts

A life is built by words of kindness
placed with cosmic timing
by those of gentle hearts.

One by one you build the steps
upon which a fragile soul
regains its strength and courage.

Like mortar between the cracks,
love holds humanity together
despite the quakes of history.

Traffic Jammer

He ain't trying to ignore ya.
He's just lost in tuneuphoria.
His head is bobbing to the beat
'cause the music sounds so sweet.

His car's got unconditioned air,
but he doesn't really care,
because he's got the radio high.
He couldn't be a happier guy.

The melody's got him in a trance.
He's just wishing he could dance.
He's your local traffic jammer.
There ain't a bigger music fan there.

He can't be bothered with road rage,
because in his head, he's on the stage,
singing along to every single word,
not caring about the speed of the herd.

Birds in Harmony

The two feathery dancers
were soaring in the wild winds,
as birds from every continent
intermingled with the stars.

The air swirled with excitement
for the concert was about to begin.
Every creature for miles
could not wait to listen in.

The parrots came forth to the front,
announcing the start of the show,
in every language of the world
that they happened to know.

Soon the skies were a bloom with music
as the birds held their springtime show,
singing about their many journeys
from the mountains to the sea.

In the houses and grassy fields below,
all the critters gathered to listen in,
and many minds were left dreaming
of travel, dazzled by the lyrics, you know.

Every song that they whistled
honored a world so wide and free,
each note a taste of paradise,
for anyone who did hear.

They sang of tall fruit orchards,
ocean waters, and city parks.
They sang ever so soulfully,
until the sunset faded into dark.

Each One of Us

Have you ever felt different?
Have you ever just felt out of place?

Do you feel like an alien
with customs from outer space?
Or maybe like an angel
who is slowly falling from grace?

You're just trying to be yourself,
but you're always going against the grain.
You aren't trying to rebel,
but you can't stand to see others in pain.

You try to join in with the team,
but it seems like you're swimming up stream.
You keep on following your dream,
but some days you just want to scream.

It turns out you're a leader,
but no one else is following.

It's that chasm of distance
that makes you see what you see.
Don't box yourself in like them,
for you were meant to be free.

Non-conformists are just
leaders without entourages.
It's amazing what one can do
if authenticity is encouraged.

Dreams Demand

It isn't so much that you follow your dreams,
but that your dreams follow you,
demanding your attention.

Go Down Easy

You want a life
that slides down smooth and sugary,
but around that curve
is a moment you couldn't see,
bouncing you around erratically
like a shiny pinball
until you understand
that life
cannot be controlled at all.

Dragonfly Tomorrows & Dog-eared Yesterdays
D.L. Lang

Yes

Life is magic
if you know where to look.

Weaving your own tales
into an incredible book.

Gushing with gratitude
for each good day.

The trick
is getting
out of the way,

for "yes"
is all you have to say,

and new doors
will open
every day.

A Circle of Dreams

We stood in a circle
of joyous possibility,
inhaling the skies,
as the sun descended
into a sea of orange
marmalade, toasting
to one another,
dreaming of fantastic futures.

The Sixties

We were more than just hippies,
artfully clad in paisley and beads,
dancing in circles, hugging trees,
for in these short years,
we brought about revolutions, peacefully.

We made pilgrimage
to North Beach and Greenwich Village
and settled in the Haight,
making music about this world's fate.

Joining hands, united by songs,
we dreamed of a time where we all got along—
an evolution of humanity,
where each and every soul could live free.

As we lazed upon the grasses,
we took every journey of the mind,
sought out all the truth we could find,
rediscovering ancient spirituality,
while forging the way for a brand new reality.

We explored traditions beyond our family,
seeking out new ways to be,
loving, living, communally,
surrounded by nature's endless beauty.

We marched together in harmony,
people gathered together as vast as the sea,
fighting for our brothers and sisters to be free—
free from Jim Crow's tyranny.

We stood up against an unjust war,
questioning just what we were fighting for.
Linked our arms together with strangers,
united for justice and peace.

Dragonfly Tomorrows & Dog-eared Yesterdays
D.L. Lang

As a generation came together,
this great nation changed forever,
inching closer towards a dream.

Dragonfly Tomorrows & Dog-eared Yesterdays
D.L. Lang

Lift Off!

Mothers, fathers, daughters, and sons
romping around in the sweet summer sun,
gazing at paintings and sculptures that won,
and creating memories for years to come.

Faces erupting in huge, silly grins,
wrapped in the awe of experience,
exploring centuries old traditions,
and trying fascinating new inventions.

Preserving the artistry of yesterday,
quilting and canning is here to stay.
Decked out in ribbons of red and blue
farm animals happily call out to you.

Couples walk the fairgrounds hand in hand,
enjoying the notes flowing from the bandstand.
Fried food fragrance fills the air,
informing your nose that it's at the fair.

Glowing rides illuminate the midway
as families unite in fun for a day.
Fireworks ignite a summertime sky,
as the Ferris wheel turns, oh, so high.

Kids try their luck at games of chance.
Winning toy prizes sparks a joyful dance.
Folks cheer loudly as the animals race.
There's something so magic about this place.

Yes, it's that amazing time of year again,
when you can let the fun shine in!
Why are you just standing there, son?
C'mon! Lift off! The fair has begun!

Dixon May Fair

When we went down to Dixon
for California's oldest fair,
there were so many goings-on
that joy floated in the air.

From the bray of the livestock
to the sounds of a country band,
this old country faire clocks
in as one of the finest in the land.

Waterfront Observations

On the waterfront flags are wavin'.
Flags from every state in the nation
just saying hello to the folks on vacation.

Workers head off to their vocations,
as fishermen reel up their crustaceans,
and families spend time in relaxation.

Joggers pause for some hydration.
Diners drink up their sweet libations.
Travelers get a fix of caffeination.

Fans cheer teams with pure elation
gathered in weekly convocation,
journeying from the ferry station.

Gentlemen engage in conversation,
as children frolic across vegetation,
and artists dream up new creations.

Where the river's flowing in separation,
gentle souls sit deep in meditation
lost in a world of contemplation.

As pigeons practice their levitation,
seagulls soar into higher elevations
passing by ghosts of the naval station.

Island Poem

It's a nice place for dreaming
in the middle of your day.

It's gonna get you scheming
towards a brand new way.

It's a place for listening
for what your soul may say.

It's a place for reminiscing
as your memories fade away.

It's a space for whistling
as you go on your way.

It's a peaceful respite
from a busy day.

I'm glad I wandered
the island today.

Generation Transformation

A generation
defined by exploration
transformed a nation.

All I've Got Left of You

We used to be so close.
We used to have heroes.
Now all I've got left of you
are these faded old photos.

We used to live to create.
We used to dream about fate.
Now all I've got left of you
are some papers in a crate.

We used to play in the streets.
We used to laugh so hard.
Now all I've got left of you
are decades old birthday cards.

We used to quote funny movies.
We used to sing with the radio.
Now all I've got left of you
are memories of years ago.

We used to have sleepovers.
We used to write our poems.
Now all I've got left of you
is this dirty headstone.

Dragonfly Tomorrows & Dog-eared Yesterdays
D.L. Lang

Time Overdrawn

Spending so much time looking forward,
ignoring the moments in which we live,
juicing our lives for all it would give.

Now the years are passing. Getting faster.
We were looking forward to experiences.
Now we're looking back at memories.

Regretting what cannot be undone.
Wishing we'd had a little bit more fun.
It's a wonder we met at all. Priorities wrong.
One day you were here. Now you're gone.

Years spent running after things.
Never stopping to laugh and sing.
Running in circles until we slide into the grave.
When's the last time you stopped to wave?

Stuck on the hamster wheel, wondering, "What's the deal?"
If you don't slow down, you're never gonna heal.
'cause bigger the wound, the more you need to feel.

Bright Light

There's a bright light coming around the bend.
That train's coming.
Gonna take me out of here.
My heart.
She's ready to run away, oh, dear.
There's a bright light coming round the bend.

There's a bright light coming around the bend.
Oh, lord.
Ain't gonna shed me any more tears.
For sure.
That train'll get me away from my fears.
There's a bright light coming round the bend.

Hanukah Train

This train's fueled by spirit, not by power nor by might.
Passing through the countryside, she's shining holy lights.
Nothing can stop her, she's going all through the night.

She's an eight car hammer running through the mountains.
Hobos are jumping up just as fast as they can get in.
The last car's left open, cause it's meant for them to stay in.

Blessings are sung soulfully as every passenger watches.
The dining car is busily serving up mountains worth of latkes.
Kids are spinning dreidels and unwrapping their new tchotchkes.

One car down you can hear the musicians praying and playing.
Hebrew, English, Yiddish, folks are singing, dancing, swaying.
This car's so packed with joy, and much more'll find its way in.

Each car's glowing brightly, lit by the flames of the menorah.
Loving families gather closely, happily studying the Torah.
There's plenty of room inside, 'cause we even saved a seat for ya.

Blanton-Kiowa Line

From Blanton up to Kiowa ran the Santa Fe,
her whistles lay silent to this very day.
It all started in 1902 by the DE&G,
stretching across the land just as far as you could see.

Passing through the towns that dotted the Great Plains,
she carried many a man and grain,
transporting stories of love and pain,
even running up those Great Salt Plains.

For ninety odd years, her tracks, they sang
as the street crossing bells, so sweetly they rang,
where the Rock Island line once met the Santa Fe,
greeting passengers as they went on their way.

Bought up by K&E back in 1997,
this line ceased to be—gone to train track heaven.
Old maps and books alone now speak of her station.
Her tool house leaves no trace of its foundation.

Her bridges have now fallen into the river.
No more freight shall she deliver.
The line still vivisects the landscape—
a scarred reminder of past escapes.

The land is divided by a barrier of green—
a line of trees that once shielded folks from the heat
slices through squares of red dirt, hay, and wheat.
In this land that once tilled itself to dust,
only a few tracks remain, just left to rust.

Now no one remembers ole W.B. Blanton,
nor the big white sign for his namesake junction.
He worked the rails from the south to the west,
once touted in the papers as one of the best.

Dragonfly Tomorrows & Dog-eared Yesterdays
D.L. Lang

When you're out walking that Northern Exposure Trail,
just remember the story of these mighty rails.
If they could only talk, the stories they'd surely tell
of the Blanton-Kiowa line that once ran so swell.

Enid

The town in which I came of age
still imprints upon this very page.
Her name translates to soul,
and upon mine she oft doth pull.

Named after an idyll itself,
her history sits upon my shelf.
Enid's dubbed appropriately
from her railroads to her prairie.

The city of my youth has changed
with many buildings rearranged.
Childhood haunts fade into the past
alongside schoolmates who have passed.

No matter the years that I am gone,
upon her stories I am oft drawn.
Hometown for me she may always be,
but I can only visit her in my memory.

Sunrise

Sippin' on an orange soda.
Just tryin' to get to know ya.

We stayed up until the sunrise.
I couldn't stop gazing in your eyes.

In those moments I remembered why.

Praying for Rain

The blistering sun
has transformed this room
into an oven.

I lie drenched upon my bed
with thoughts of past summers
floating in my head.

Roasting whilst traversing
the airbase pool.
No air conditioning
at my high school.

Hanging wet towels
on a backyard clothesline.
Pushing the lawnmower
in bright, hot sunshine.

Staying up all night
to avoid the scorching heat.
Running through sprinklers
with my bare feet.

Going for a joyride
with the AC on full blast.
Overheating my car
for such comfort couldn't last.

Catching hailstones
in a freak summer storm,
when moments before
it was swelteringly warm.

Dragonfly Tomorrows & Dog-eared Yesterdays
D.L. Lang

Memories are seared
upon my brain.
If you want to be cooler,
you've got to pray for rain.

April Foolery

April fools may bring us flowers.
Bunnies lay eggs to be devoured.
Holidays revive ancient traditions.
Poets inscribe lines of inspiration.

Penguins party internationally.
Israelites were freed from slavery.
The spring moon, it wanes and waxes,
as couples argue about their taxes.

Tales are told of human be-in's past,
as rebels publicly enjoy the grass.
We honor our dear mother earth.
Protesters remind leaders of its worth.

Many wars across April in history.
Maybe next April we'll have peace.
We spend a day planting new trees,
while sneezing from our allergies.

Athletes now run their marathons.
Look at that. April's almost gone.

Anytime

Anytime that I miss you,
I just turn on a record.
Away into the night floats any discord,
melting away with every sweet chord.

Sittin' down by the lake,
I wonder if I've made a big mistake.
As I watch the merry go round,
children's laughter the only sound.

Gazing at the sunset as it peaks through the trees.
Each branch is gently waving in the breeze.
An elegant dance performed by every leaf.

Hunting in my car,
trying to find the right map.
Ain't it amazing just how much crap
we carry in our hearts?

The seeds of evolution
are contained in the roots,
for you must know where you come from
in order to make the right moves.

Hang On to Your Soul

A soul is a force
so powerful
that it cannot be
forever contained
in the same place,
let alone
in the same body.

A soul speaks
with a voice
beyond time,
if only we dare
to listen.

A soul may be
immersed in wisdom
beyond its keeper.

Art is a manifestation
of the soul,
aiming for growth
before returning home.

Sally

My first doggy had curls as black as charcoal,
but even more beautiful was her sweet soul.
My Sally, dear Sally, how I loved her so!
I met her when I was just three years old.

Forever, forever, my heart, she stole
with sweet puppy kisses worth more than gold.
Oh Sally, dear Sally, I watched her get old.
Together like sisters, we both did grow.

I shall never forget that fourth of July.
The loss of our canine—torrents we did cry!
My Sally, dear Sally, she ran off in fright
as fireworks crackled on that clear Texas night.

Many family dogs have since come to play,
joining my dear Sally in my heart these days,
but the love of such a gentle friend never fades.
Having known a dog's love, we are left changed.

The Talebearer

She thinks she knows everything
to be known about the world,
but she's really just projecting,
behaving like a teenage girl.

She jumps to conclusions
about everyone she sees.
She repeats all the rumors
that she hears of you and me.

She won't confront you
about what it is she hears,
but she'll spread around stories
that'd have you in tears.

Rather than truth seeking,
her mind fills in the gaps,
but rest assured everything
she says is a just load of crap.

Zing

When life has ceased to have that zing,
seek out joy and try new things
in order to find what makes your heart sing.

Leave the familiar for some place new.
Maybe bring a good friend with you.
Listen to your heart. It knows what to do.

A refreshed soul you shall then find
living beyond the daily grind,
for novelty expands the mind.

A Home

I get so tired
spending these many hours
all alone,

when it's your voice
and your face
that makes
this house a home.

I keep wandering
around this world,
gazing up the skies,

but there's no place
I feel more loved
than when
I gaze into your eyes.

One Two

One. Two. Feelin' blue.
What to do. Up to you.
Slow down. Rainy day.
Low down. Nothin' in my way.
Hold on. Layin' in my bed.
Cold dawn. Nothin' to be said.
Hot tea. Whistlin' on the stove.
Coffee. Headin' to the grove.
Walkin'. Got to clear my mind.
Talkin'. Time to hit rewind.
Gazing. Lost in the starry night.
Lazin'. Everything'll be alright.
Hold on. Love is a shining light.
Dream on. Don't give up the fight.

Somewhere Beyond

I've got cabin fever.
I'm waiting for something to relieve her.

I'm sick of staring at the paper.
I'm worried 'bout this nation.
What's gonna save her?

I'm tired of lying in my bed,
escaping into the mind corridors
that I've seen so many times before.
I'd rather be hiking instead.

I'm wrapped inside these melodies.
My head's somewhere beyond,
just yearning to be free.

Personal Evolution

Just because you know biographical facts
doesn't mean that you know anyone's full story.
Just because they may have said it in the past
doesn't mean that they will always be for it.

We all run into experiences that change us.
Nobody is perfect and assuming so is dangerous.
We all warble between certitude and naïveté.
We all accidentally hurt one another on some days.

Life is a journey of personal transformation.
Before you condemn someone examine all the information.
Don't hold a person liable for their youthful misgivings.
As adults we all must learn how to be more forgiving.

It is up to every soul on earth to seek out evolution.
To grow beyond the events that leave our world polluted.
We all must try to become more wise and empathetic.
To leave a positive mark upon the world and not regret it.

We all have our moments where we may miss the mark,
but that doesn't mean that we must remain in the dark.
Admit it when you have done someone wrong,
then find the inner strength to just move right along.

Give everyone you know the benefit of the doubt.
Not everyone's mistakes are worthy of being kicked out.
Look for consistency in each person's life long behavior.
The point is to do your best before you hit the graveyard.

Like Broken Glass

Like broken glass
washed up on the beach…

Like a shipwreck
come up from the sea…

Here I landed.

Here is me.

Moments

I wish words
could capture
the beauty of
this moment,

but moments
are meant
to be free.

Old Songs

And to think
I thought
these words
were about the past,

and not some
imagined future
now present.

Prophetic words
cut through the dust of memory
as the wheel of time rolls on,
repeating history
until we learn.

Melodies ring out
under the glow of the neon
whispering timeless wisdom,

but are you listening?

Sparked by Melody

Sparked by melody
borne after the catalyst
of community,

I have travelled
to the opposite plane
from whence I began,

and whilst memories
hang onto my heart,
I wish to remain
in this new evolution,

for while it is shaky,
and I know not
what is to come,

it is, somehow, better
to go through
than to remain stagnant,

better to be tested,
than to never learn.

Renewed

I reach out my hand
in a prayer, yearning,
for the kind of peace
and joy that the world
cannot penetrate.

In return, you hand me
the gift of songs
sung with friends,
a respite from
life's demands.

Renewed.

Whole again.

Awe

When awe
has you stopped
in your tracks,

then you know
that you can never
turn back.

Oh, no,
you can never turn back.

As the Sun

A country hillside
landscape of green
with brightly colored
flowers dotting the scene.

Beneath the blur of the trees,
the sun, it dapples
through the leaves.

Beneath the mighty sky so wide
roads weave worlds together beside
rural fences demarcating home.

Street Mouse

A mouse sunbathing
on hot concrete, rolling like
a pup, belly up.

Class Participation

The extravert model of education
seems to be the rapid dissemination
of several hundred factoids of information
followed by a demand for instant observations.

This only leaves this introvert frustrated
as we need time to process the data
before we can have anything to say to ya,
and sometimes that may be days later.

Give me one on one instruction,
or lose me in deep conversation,
allow me to take notation,
and spend days lost in reflection
instead of expecting instant gratification.

Beachside

The ocean sings her mighty songs
for any heart her tune will calm.

Seagulls circle in bluest skies
as particles of sand race at high tide.

Couples stroll along side by side
as children build their castles high.

Some may picnic beneath umbrellas
as sunbathers catch the eyes of fellas.

Dogs play chicken with the waves
as surfers get the rush they crave.

Lighting campfires at ocean side,
friends bond well into the night.

People arrive from far and wide,
for every moment is worth the ride.

A Napa Moment

I hear that wine train as she's rollin' down the road.
She's such a fine train just carrying her load.
I admire her steel wagons as her horn so sweetly blows.
The notes sound beautiful fillin' up the summer air.
Diners drink until they're full of wine country fare.

Mall Walker

Dressed for morning marathons,
I snake around on cool tile,
ignoring the bark of salesmen,
dodging hordes of well-dressed
teenagers: the native species
of the retail jungle.

I drink from
cool, clear chlorinated fountains,
as fragrances of world cuisine
blend together in the stale air
with perfume-laden department stores,

whilst wishing I was out on a trail
far away from the lure of sales
of things I care not to own.

epic history poem

A writer truly learns by doing.
Life throws you down a flight of stairs
and then asks you to tell that story,
half-stoned, one-armed and no pants,
listening to country.

You followed every rule,
but Murphy's law governs your life.
The past only predicts future behavior
if you expect consistency,
but nothing ever is, as far as I can see.

A poet is the only role
that doesn't feel like an audition.
Figure out who you're meant to be
and break with stale traditions.

As the sun paints patterns upon the wall,
you sit desperately trying not to feel at all,
for inside one teardrop you feel hurricanes.
Stay content to drift to the log cabin in your mind
where boredom is merely the freedom to daydream.

Mama made angels out of clothespins
daddy drew doodles,
grandma shook a plastic bag
just to make you smile,
for you are just a child forever lost to the wind.

You don't learn to swim by listening
to the voice that says you'll drown.
Synchronize with your inner compass.
Orient your ears to the whisperings of your soul.
Solitude is the fertilizer of brilliance.
While they debate, you contemplate.

Dragonfly Tomorrows & Dog-eared Yesterdays
D.L. Lang

TV portrays no realism; no resemblance to real life,
only a thousand ways of expressing nothing.
Spend more time staring into space
than watching what's his face
provide daily enumeration
of events that cause frustration.

Staring out the back window whilst sipping soda,
you're left intoxicated by sun rays that dance with palm trees,
and peak between mid-century tract homes
with stone veneer for exterior castle ambiance,
igniting visions of well crafted images
of Capri clad housewives with cigarette holders
blindly driveling on about some first world problem
with now comically outdated technology—
a split second flashback to a film
indulged once upon a teenage snow day
where palm trees seemed like paradise,
but so does every place.

Rather than be content in your blessings,
you go through life with tinsel town perceptions,
framing your life by a caricature of perfection,
comparing yourself to a shallow cartoon,
stumbling towards dreams not your own,
until the day you pull out a microscope
to reexamine the circumference of your own wanderings,
recalibrating your own character development,
discovering the joy of eternal mystery.
Let your mind take you to the places
that your feet will never reach.

Dragonfly Tomorrows & Dog-eared Yesterdays
D.L. Lang

Would that it be more comedy than tragedy
in the final tally.
The what ifs will haunt you.
The cruelty of hindsight.
It will taunt you daily,
asking why you so denied yourself for so long,
until you take the steps to change.

Practicality and frugality is lethal to progress,
burying living dreams
in bureaucratic ash,
the remains of steps untaken
as so often we bow
to the tyranny of the easy,
and forsake our own hearts
until its too late to chase after desire.

Find a way to move beyond
into the sweet embrace of possibility,
infinite and comfortably uncomfortable,
swimming towards a life well lived.

The happy accident of your love
birthed a longing to rise into the clouds,
orbit the sun and dance with the stars,
yet we are chained to the ground
rules set forth by nameless hordes
of the past.

A soul finding more value
in moral values
than market values
needs moments of meaning
as much as breathing.

Dragonfly Tomorrows & Dog-eared Yesterdays
D.L. Lang

Home is the eye of the hurricane,
a calm connection,
but you cannot stay there forever
if you want to see the rainbows.

I'd like to think for some fleeting moments,
I touched happiness
on some stages
and between these pages,
despite not earning wages.

These hands that once spoke for me
in cryptic rhyme,
trapped now as they may be
unearthed the voice
who shall roar forth forever.

Poetry is the instruction manual for existence.
Infinite metaphors. Results may vary.
Do not try this at home. Carries no cash.

Creativity is the voice of an angel
sheltering a broken heart
as it heals.
Every creation like a desert rain.

A penguru swims the sea,
catching fish in pouch,
dispensing wisdom.

Faith is a boomerang.
You will feel far.
You will feel close.
You will feel far again.

Dragonfly Tomorrows & Dog-eared Yesterdays
D.L. Lang

Music is the glue of life,
connecting generations
as each moment in history
is orbiting around a song
woven into memory.

And so home is a song,
a prayer, a poem,
crying out for something better,
a world beyond authoritarian designs,
beyond rigid timelines,
something more divine,
a place beyond time,
loving and kind.

Antisocial Media

I'm tired of these corporations
that monitor private conversations
amid advertisements for vacations.

There is a lack of communication
that merely leads to the degradation
of once vibrant relations,
when real life interactions
are replaced with frustration.

We've become our representations,
voyeurs of vapid preoccupations,
sharing only other's creations,
whilst lacking in imagination.

I've no longer the motivation
to make my daily contribution:
a vain offering of information
in the name of connection.

The Way to Contentment

Don't let your wants
become a burden,
for you must find joy
in the striving.

Wracked with a sour nostalgia,
riding the comparison carousel
at the competition carnival
is no way to succeed.

Worry is a well-worn carpet.
Failure is just a synonym
for "try again."

Humanity

We are bound together
like flower petals—

each distinct,
yet connected—

planted together
in the gardens of relationship,

confidently unique,
yet harmoniously as one,

orbiting our shared humanity,
woven together in
some floral tapestry
across the earth.

Brightest

Said just about all I can say,
and I said it yesterday.

Wandering on through the fray,
I think I best be on my way.

You might call it genius
while others proclaim weirdness.

I'm just searching for a hint of bliss
before I leave this wilderness.

I'm gonna sing my way
through the apocalypse,
for lights, they shine brightest
in the darkness.

Dragonfly Tomorrows & Dog-eared Yesterdays
D.L. Lang

Greed's Disconnect

They'll judge you for your possessions
that you purchased before the recession.
They'll have no sympathy for your depression,
but you cannot afford a therapy session.

They'll start wars over resources
while wasting more over the course of it.
They'll cut funding for living artists
while paying millions for ancient artwork.

They'll cut housing subsidies
as they live in mansions with unused rooms.
They'll expect you to live on fast food
while refusing to pay them well too.

They'll cut food stamps
as they dine on single meals costing thousands.
They'll cut public education
while sending their kids to expensive schools.

They'll blame the poor for not saving
as they waste millions on frivolity.
They'll tell you to do it yourself
while they don't even drive, cook, or clean.

They'll tell you to get a low wage job
while they laze about in luxury.
They'll cut public transit funding
as they ride around in limousines.

They'll only donate to foundations
as men lie in the gutter in starvation.
They won't fund universal healthcare,
but God forbid you ever cut theirs.

Dragonfly Tomorrows & Dog-eared Yesterdays
D.L. Lang

They call themselves job creators
while only giving themselves raises.
They hate paying their taxes,
but wouldn't last a day in a lower bracket.

Although

Though we might drown in sea of blues
by immersion in the daily news,

the hope upon which we must cling
is infused within the songs we sing,
for tomorrow, it shall surely begin.

So long as we step forth, we win.

Keep minds aloft in dreams renewed,
for fear dictates not what dreamers do,
and dictators, they are mortals, too.

Ochlocracy

Keep your wits about you
when out among the crowd.

Your passion for an issue
may make you scream aloud,

but succumbing to mob rule
may not leave you feeling proud.

Politics

A never-ending chess match.
Alone we are pawns.
Together we are invincible.

This Earth Day

God's children flood the streets
to honor their mother earth,
spending hours upon their feet
to remind government of its real worth.

Stay Lit

Sometimes, candles
struggle to stay lit
when the wind blows hardest.

Overwhelmed by darkness,
pitch black, unable to see
the path forward.

One by one,
watching the lights retire
when they are needed most.

Leave your light on
as long as you can,
and when it gets heavy,
just take my hand.

I'll carry the torch
to remind you of your fire
until we become the inferno
that powers the sunrise
of a better day across this land.

On Fear

If you choose to self-censor,
to cover your own beautiful voice
that heretofore rang out
in favor of freedom and justice,
then you are doing their work
for them.

Do not let fear ensnare you
like a snake, strangling
your conscience.

Turn your anger
into the fires of confidence.

You shall find yourself
surrounded by friends—
souls who shall fight
until the nightmare ends.

Lines

There are poets hiding in the newspapers,
regurgitating rhyme from the headlines,
the daily spin cycle of our times,
deciphering inner monologues of personal madness
whose only catalyst is our collective sadness
when measuring the gap:

the gap between here and heaven,
between here and perfection,
between here and kindergarten,
between here and graduation,
between here and the coffin,
between here and disappointment,
between what is said or held in,
between here and the illusions

once held together by what we thought,
nay, nay, what we were taught,
that this country stood for,
swallowing our youthful minds,
silenced by boredom and repetition,
swallowing any questions,
ignoring the lump in the throat of intuition,
in relation to the betrayal of our values,

shielded by those who stand together,
shouting into the stratosphere,
standing upon hope with a hint of fear,
among the murmur of the crowds,
thinking in unison, thinking out loud,
carrying what ifs and future generations,
perhaps, never to come into existence,

Dragonfly Tomorrows & Dog-eared Yesterdays
D.L. Lang

multiplied by the number of text books
we once lugged around
only to be told one version of the past
now shattered by the truth,

leaving us scrambling to measure
what's left of pleasure
in times like these,
in times of hard realities,
etched in tablets of poetry

never to be read
by those who need its ecstasy,
by those who need its influence,
by those who need drink its truth,
by those who need hear it,
by those who could move mountainsides
sparked by broadsides,
by those who need read it the most,

instead left drowning behind coffee stained teeth,
never to meet the pages of chapbooks,
nor exiting chapped lips,
slowly dancing upon cigarette smoke,
to be snuffed out by too many bagels,
and left smoldering in the letter boxes of yesteryear.

Dragonfly Tomorrows & Dog-eared Yesterdays
D.L. Lang

instead the greatest minds
sit analyzing the rhymes
weaved into popular song lines
about sand, and gin, and lime,
lifestyles of shrimp, and gold, and wine,
about unrecognizable times,
had by the unattainable slime
that walk upon a poor man's spine,
scolding them not to whine,
as they ascend the throne of our times,
leaving us only with headlines,
swimming around the spin cycle,
searching for the meaning we left behind.

Dear Land of the Free

I've got one foot in Jamestown,
and another on the plane I came in on.
I've got a unit of ancestral infantry,
and roots stretching back to royalty.

I'm related to presidents,
great explorers, and kings,
poets, revolutionaries,
and those who soulfully sing.

I sit perched on the wall,
ever so precariously,
between the world and citizenry.

When you say immigrant,
you're talking about me,
but my ancestors are firmly rooted
in the fabric of this country.
I would not exist without
the service they gave to thee.

When you attack immigrants,
you're aiming right at me.
What the hell happened,
dear land of the free?

IWWD

It's a beautiful day for a strike,
standing up for women's rights.

On the waterfront we stood,
in the name of sisterhood.

A sea of solidarity clad in red,
just like our foremothers did.

What if?

The day the warriors went on strike
billions of young folks refused to fight,
as they looked into each other's eyes
saw only the other soul's light.

Their weapons were just left to lie
out of brotherly love and not from fright,
for they refused to kill and to die,
leaving their families no reason to cry.

Radioactive Returns

The relics of fallout shelters
lying dormant in high school halls,
relegated to preservation
in peculiar propaganda PSAs,
rusty yellowed warning signs,
and flashback fifties films,
as time transformed,
teachers talked tornado drills—
cover your head
and head for the hills!

Thoughts of
nuclear annihilation
were meant
to stay in dusty volumes
of cold war inspired thrillers,
and historical tales
from previous war time killings—
how horrifying
the consequences,
yet countries
during seasons
of fashionable tyranny,
lust openly
for this destruction,
as if mutually assured devastation
were somehow easier
than negotiation,
forgetting the lessons
of previous generations—
too costly an education.

Dragonfly Tomorrows & Dog-eared Yesterdays
D.L. Lang

Could the nukes just fade
into the past
like purple copier ink,
and decaying educational film strips,
wormholes slowly eating images
like a buffet of memories,
fading out
with the tangles and tangles
of out of sync cassette soundtracks,
as if they too outlived their
usefulness—
a technology declared passé
by a newly evolved humanity
aiming for a better world?

....or merely still having one.

Cats on Caravan

Cats are on caravan,
crossing rivers and mountains.

Roaring for freedom.

Claws out, if necessary.

New Old America

Awake. A week.
In this new old America.
denial of proven reality.
belief in repeated lies.
division by identities.
silencing of the smartest.
omission of history.
blind favor of partisanship.
irrational hatred spewed.
well dressed bullies.
nauseating headlines.
saddened our faces.
elimination of beauty in public spaces.
signing of edicts from high places.
causing questioning of status.

Awake! not weak!
this ain't new America.
rebellion of the truth.
solidarity of humanity.
standing firm on values.
refusal of blind acceptance.
holding hands of strangers.
creation of movements.
gathering for goodness.
justice will be won.
signs of hope in weary fists.
people rising to the challenge.
Among them. here! belonging.

Immigrants' Truth

It is becoming quite clear
that you don't want me here,
but I refuse to live in fear,
nor let your rhetoric reduce me to tears.

For the elements of my identity,
that are unchangeable,
that make you uncomfortable,
no such words of apology
shall exit my lips.

I will not apologize for existing.
I will not apologize for who I am.
I will not apologize for living in this land.

Your birthplace
does not make
you at all superior to me,
for I am human,
and I deserve to be free.

What's It Gonna Take?

What's it gonna take before we're all awake?
What's it gonna take to have us stop the hate?
What's it gonna take before we hit the brakes?
What's it gonna take to make us truly change?

What's it gonna take to stop these petty games?
What's it gonna take to make us love again?
What's it gonna take to heal everyone's pain?
What's it gonna take to bring us hope again?

What's it gonna take to make a life more wise?
What's it gonna take to free us from the lies?
What's it gonna take to reverse this fate?
What's got to break before we see what's at stake?

Speak out even if you shake!

Not Your Problem?

"Well, it doesn't affect me,"
is not reassuring, yet instead
is the sound of your heart
swinging shut to the suffering
of your fellow humans.

You Cannot See Through Gold

There ain't wisdom in riches,
for you gather it in a pile,
creating misery being miserly,
as others starve all the while.

You care not about others
but your own family tree,
while your sisters and brothers
are yearning to be free.

You'd rather roll back progress
than take responsibility,
but then, well, I guess,
that would take humility.

You've got no idea
how the rest of us live,
for you cannot see
with a heart so stiff.

Your notion of life
is surely lacking soul
for you only cause strife
when money is your goal.

Learn to see with your heart
what you cannot with your eyes.
Learn to research the truth,
for you're just spreading lies.

You got to act out of service
for that is your true duty
instead of just paying lip service
and then acting so rudely.

Dragonfly Tomorrows & Dog-eared Yesterdays
D.L. Lang

Nah, I don't despise you,
for I know why you're blind.
You ain't got nothing but your
own interests on your mind.

Dragonfly Tomorrows & Dog-eared Yesterdays
D.L. Lang

Where are the Heroes?

We are the lawyers showing up to airports.
We are the regular people showing up to our first protests.
We are the people giving our first donations to the ACLU.
We are the people who ran for delegations for the first time.
We are the journalists who are continuing to write the truth.
We are the celebrities who are risking fandom by speaking out.
We are the artists who refused to play the inauguration.
We are the taxi drivers who went on strike.
We are the students who walked out of school in protest.
We are the teachers training the next generations.
We are the people who walked out of jobs in protest.
We are the government employees refusing immoral orders.
We are the musicians crying out in protest songs.
We are the poets bearing witness, sparking hope.
We are those who continue to treat humanity with dignity.
We are those who choose morality over harsh legality,
and we are more visible now than at any other time.
We are choosing to be the heroes that we seek.
We are millions, and this darkness, we shall defeat.
We shall resist, we shall persist, and stop the madness.

Affirmations of a Dream

I still believe that
humanity is
inherently loving...

that that love
is what governs
the soul...

that the soul
is the compass
pointing towards
the heart...

that that heart
beats steady
towards a dream...

that that dream
will be realized
by our unity...

that these actions of unity
will bring forth a time of peace...

for we simply cannot
continue the paths
of greed, that only breed
suffering and turmoil,
wars over gold and for oil...

we must cease to robotically pursue
these ancient visions of division
set by long dead eyes left blinded by hatred,
planned in minds soured by frustration,

Dragonfly Tomorrows & Dog-eared Yesterdays
D.L. Lang

yet the clown emperor, he is naked,
behind old flags still waving,
with old beliefs oft left unshaken

for here we stand,
pledging allegiance to a nation
built on idealistic foundations,
left cracked by the weight of hypocrisy...

a nation built on the backs of the invisible,
whose voices were long silenced,
and who now cry out with wisdom
against the tyranny of a flawed system...

no, we can no longer ignore
that for which we have waited,
that for which we are fated,
on this day we must awaken,
for history is ours for the making,

but we must rise to take it
for the hour is growing later,
and clocks are meant
to move forward,
and freedom, freedom is not
easily forgotten once tasted...

we, we are the majority!
we are the ones who care!
we haven't the time for despair!
nay, with every passing second,
we must affirm our hope!

in hardship or opportunity,
from the country to the city,
our unity must build up community...

Dragonfly Tomorrows & Dog-eared Yesterdays
D.L. Lang

empowered by kindness,
leaping in faith or faithless,
we shall fight until all are free!

moving through all tragedy,
all together, you and me,
until that dream is reached:

an eternal guarantee
that every earthly soul is assured
a life of dignity
simply by its existence.

Printed in Great Britain
by Amazon